# Utrec

# Two-day tour of Utrecht: the smaller, less touristy Amsterdam!

By Aly Coy

## Help us keep this guide up to date

We make every effort to make sure the facts and information in this itinerary are accurate and up to date. However, changes can and will occur. (This is part of what makes travel so interesting, of course.) This can be something as small as a phone number or hours of operations changing, or as significant as a new attraction opening.

We would love to hear from you if you notice any discrepancies in the itinerary, or if you have any suggestions on how to improve. All comments and suggestions will be communicated to the author and included in our regular updating process.

**Please send any and all feedback to hello@unanchor.com.**

Thank you and happy travelling!

Copyright © 2021 by Unanchor LLC

All rights reserved. No part of this publication may be reproduced, distributed, or transmitted in any form or by any means, including photocopying, recording, or other electronic or mechanical methods, without the prior written permission of the publisher, except in the case of brief quotations embodied in critical reviews and certain other noncommercial uses permitted by copyright law. For permission requests, write to the publisher, addressed "Attention: Permissions Coordinator," at the address below.

All maps are copyright OpenStreetMap contributors. Please visit www.openstreetmap.org/copyright for more information.

**Address:**

Unanchor
4711 Hope Valley Rd
4F - #1157
Durham, NC 27707
www.unanchor.com

**Ordering Information:**

Quantity sales. Special discounts are available on quantity purchases by corporations, associations, and others. For details, contact the publisher at the address above.

Orders by U.S. trade bookstores and wholesalers. Please contact Unanchor at hello@unanchor.com, or visit http://www.unanchor.com.

Printed in the United States of America

# Table of contents

**About the Author**     7

**Day 1**
Taking a picture of the Dom Tower     11
The Oudegracht Canal     14
Saint Catherine's Convent     17
Lunch at 't Oude Pothuys     19
University Museum and Botanical Gardens     22
Haunted Abandoned House     25
Kafe Belgie     28

**Day 2**
Graffiti Wall by Central Station     31
Flea Market     33
Mariaplaats     36
Lunch at Springhaver     40
Centraal Museum (incl. Dick Bruna Huis)     42
Dinner at ACU     45

**Appendix**

**About Unanchor**     54

**Other Unanchor Itineraries**     57

# About the Author

## Aly Coy

I'm addicted to travel and discovering new cultures and languages. I've been wandering around Europe for the last five years after studying English Literature in Nova Scotia at Dalhousie University. I started my tourism career in Halifax, Nova Scotia as a tour guide and loved showing travelers the best that the city had to offer. I was then a tour guide for my hometown of Toronto while I saved up to head to Europe. After backpacking around Western Europe for three months I found myself working at a hostel in Amsterdam and performing city walking tours. In Amsterdam I met a mix of people from around the world, all looking for something new.

The city is welcoming to the strange and obscure, and it's easy to find a niche within these things. After the year of rain and biking I craved crisp snow, so I went to the French Alps to be an au pair for five months and attempted to teach myself how to snowboard. The ski season came to an end and a feeling like I needed to see the people who I grew up with began. I spent four months back in Toronto, seeing family and old friends. I then got another job in a hostel and as a tour guide but this time in the south of Spain. Eight months later I was speaking broken Spanish and taking daily siestas. A month in India showed me a different side of life to say the least. All extremes at once mixed with 40 degree (celsius) temperatures makes you appreciate the little things, like drinking tap water for example. Saw the Daiai Lama speak, nature hikes in the mountains, eating with my hands, never been so hot and thirsty in my life, beautiful views and experiences unlike anything else.

Beginning to feel the need for stability, I planned to return to The Netherlands to the life I started two years earlier but out of the hectic city. I lived for over a year on a community farm trying to be as self sufficient as possible. There were goats and chickens to entertain us and we lived off the vegetables grown in the garden and left over from an organic grocery store. I then moved off-the-grid to The Spanish Pyrenees living in a mountain community for four months. Craving running water, electricity, and speaking English, I left the community and came back to Toronto to reconnect with old friends and to take a creative writing course through Humber College. I then moved to British Columbia where I am working and living on an organic farm, trying to find a balance between city and nature. The mix of cultures and experiences behind me has shaped my views and perspectives on life. My goal is to share as much as I have learned through writing about those life lessons.

Home Town: Toronto
Twitter: alythecoy
Blog: http://www.thecoypond.com

# Day 1

## Taking a picture of the Dom Tower

**Time:** 10:00 am ~ 10:30 am
**Type:** Place of Worship
**Address:** Domplein 21

**How to get there:** From central station, walk straight ahead on Vredenburg and right on Lange Elisabethstraat, which turns into Steenweg. On the street before the canal turn right, on Choorstraat, and left over the bridge. **If you can't find it just look up**, and most likely you'll see the Dom Toren, or ask anyone and they'll know.

## DAY 1

The **Dom Toren** (tower) is the biggest tourist attraction in the city. We'll get that out of the way first. It was built in the mid-14th century connected to the Saint Martin Cathedral. A huge storm in 1674 brought the unfinished nave crashing down, freeing the tower from the rest of the building.

Originally, it was used as a watchtower, and has on the first floor a private chapel for the Bishop of Utrecht.

Today, it's the highest church tower in The Netherlands standing at 368 feet. You can climb the 465 steps with a pre-booked guided tour for €9, but today we're just going to take a look, and a picture of the giant that watches over the city.

# Walk from Dom Toren to the Oudegracht

**Transport Type:** Walk
**Time:** 10:30 am ~ 10:35 am

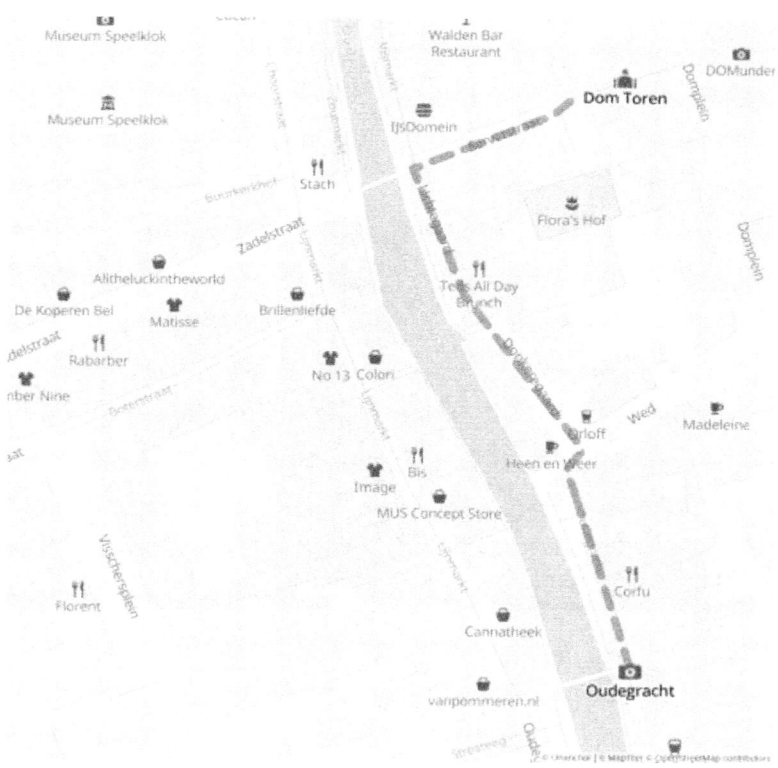

Walk in the direction of central station along Servetstraat. Take first left onto the canal Lichte Gaard, which turns into the Oudegracht Canal.

# The Oudegracht Canal

**Time:** 10:35 am ~ 11:15 am
**Type:** District
**Address:** Oudegracht

Utrecht is famous for having streets at canal level. First take a walk along the cobble stone street that lines the canal, and take a short stop in the ultra-hip second-hand vintage store **Episode**, 206 Oudegracht. It's for both men and women, and are quoted for selling "daily-wear to party clothes, from sporty to dressed-up, from freak to casual."

After spending your daily budget at Episode, take the next set of stairs down after the bridge, and experience the Oudegracht how it should be!

The **Oudegracht,** or old canal, is part of the Vecht River, that runs through the city. In 1275, the city built locks after major flooding filled the wharfs that lined the canal. Those cellar/wharfs are now turned into cafe's, shops and bars. We'll be having lunch at one of those old wharfs later on in the tour.

# Walk from Oudegracht to St. Catherine Convent

**Transport Type:** Walk
**Time:** 11:15 am ~ 11:20 am

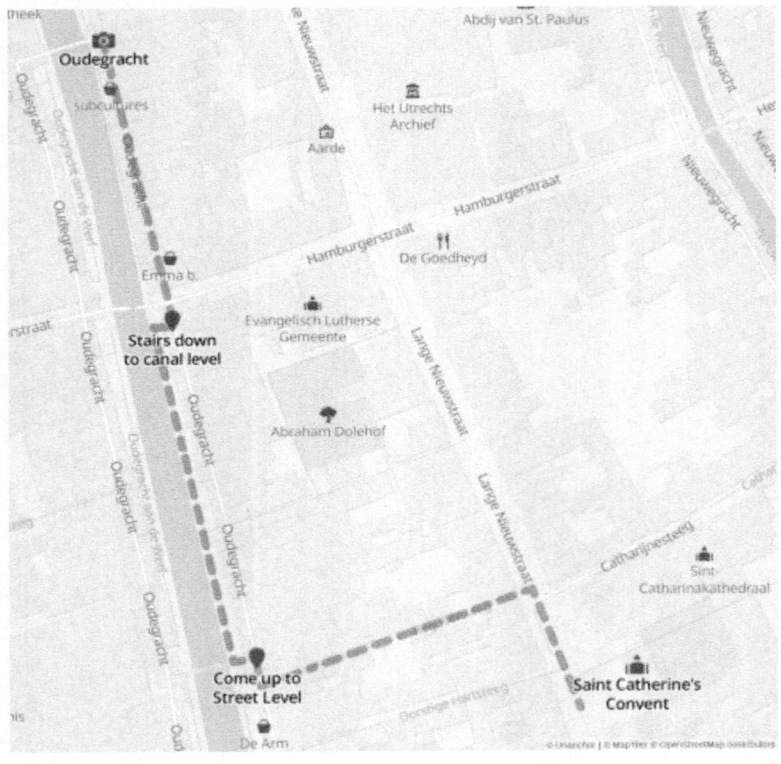

After coming up to street level, take the first left on Reguliersteeg and the first right on Lange Nieuwestraat. The Convent is on your left-hand side.

# Saint Catherine's Convent

**Time:** 11:30 am ~ 01:00 pm
**Type:** Place of Worship
**Address:** Lange Nieuwestraat 28

**Saint Catherine's Convent** was built in the 16th Century as a monastery for members of the Order of the Knights of St. John. It also acted as a teaching hospital.

It's now a museum filled with Dutch art from the Medieval period to the 21st century. There are pieces from Rembrandt and other famous Dutch artists from **The Golden age** of The Netherlands in the 16th and 17th century. During The Golden Age, the country was booming when trading around the world reached its peak. The Dutch are known for their ships sailing the seas and trading such things as exotic spices, precious metals, textiles and slaves.

# Walk to Lunch at 't Oude Pothuys

**Transport Type:** Walk
**Time:** 01:00 pm ~ 01:05 pm

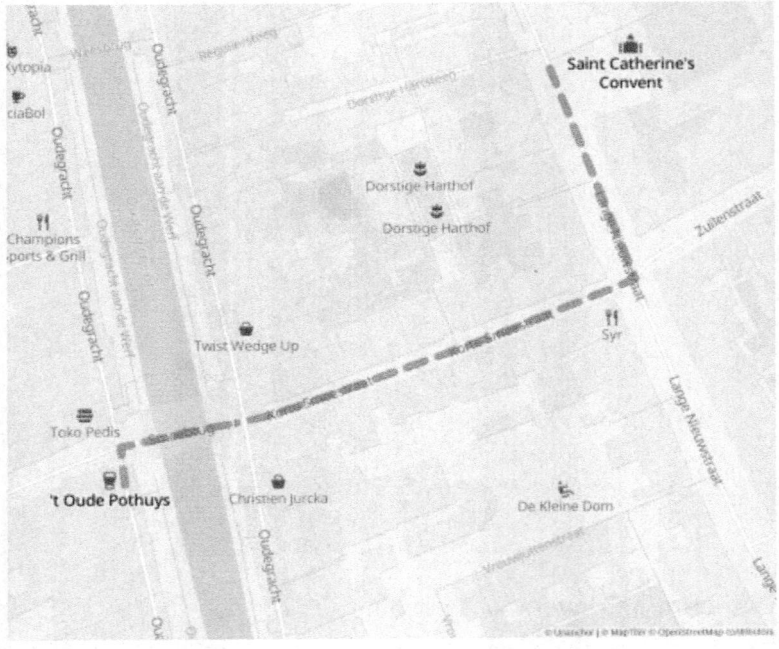

Out of the Convent, continue along Lange Nieuwestraat to Korte Smeestraat. You'll find yourself back on the Oudegracht Canal. Cross the bridge, quick left, and the 't Oude Pothuys is on the left down the stairs (there will be signs for the restaurant).

# Lunch at 't Oude Pothuys

**Time:** 01:05 pm ~ 02:15 pm
**Type:** Restaurant / Cafe / Bar
**Address:** Oudegracht 279

canal view of 't Oude Pothuys photo credit: aly coy

't Oude Pothuys, pronounced Het Ow-duh Pot House, isn't a coffeeshop to smoke weed, but a restaurant and music venue. Check out what's playing that evening while enjoying soup, sandwich or salad. Lunch is served from Wed-Sun. If you're touring on a Monday or Tuesday, head straight to the next sight, the University Museum, and have lunch in the cafe there.

**Menu suggestion:** Cheese puff pastry with salad. (Talmouse, bladerdeeg gevuld met verschillende soorten kazen uit de oven, met salade van mesclun en kastanjes € 15,25)

**Price range:** €8-€17

# Lunch to University Museum

**Transport Type:** Walk
**Time:** 02:15 pm ~ 02:30 pm

Continue along the Oudegracht and cross the first bridge on left. Continue straight from the bridge onto the street Vrouwjuttenstraat, then at the first street take a right onto Lange Nieuwestraat, you'll see the University Museum on your left.

# University Museum and Botanical Gardens

**Time:** 02:30 pm ~ 05:00 pm
**Type:** Museum
**Address:** Lange Nieuwstraat 106

The University Museum is a mix of an interactive science adventure and botanical garden. There's exhibits such as 'back to the future' where you choose your profession and see the environmental impact it will have on the earth. There is a youth lab, experimenting on the senses, a medical lab, knowledge test, the science of everyday objects from a cell phone to an agenda.

In the botanical gardens, take a step into nature, away from the city streets. Since 1723, medicinal plants and herbs mixed with exotic flowers and trees have made up the gardens. Gingko was first introduced to Europe in this specific botanical garden.

Grab a coffee at the cafe if you have time, if not, head to the next stop - the haunted house!

**24** DAY 1

# University Museum to Haunted House

**Transport Type:** Walk
**Time:** 05:00 pm ~ 05:05 pm

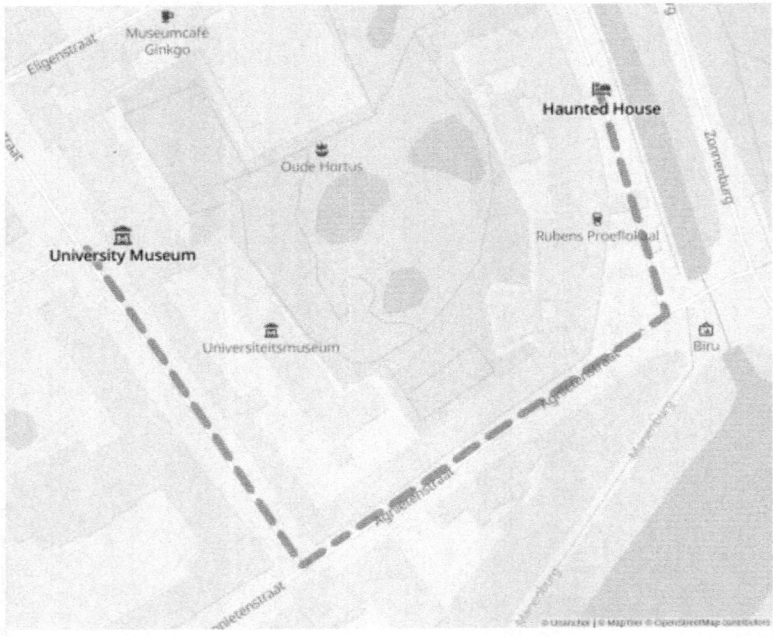

It's around the corner, so walk left out of the museum on Lange Nieuwstraat and take the first left on Agnietenstraat then another left on Nieuwegracht and it's number 193 on Nieuwegracht.

# Haunted Abandoned House

**Time:** 05:05 pm ~ 05:30 pm
**Type:** Other
**Address:** Nieuwegracht 193

See anything spooky in the windows? photo credit: Aly Coy

There are lots of rumours surrounding this house, one of them being that an exorcism was performed in 2002. The first strange occurrence was that the seemingly healthy owner suffered a heart attack in the attic. He left the house in his will to his daughter, who turned mad. She only lived in the attic where her father had died, and left the rest of the house to ruins. Half a dozen cats also lived in the house, and when the woman eventually died. There was a meter high pile of faeces found in the kitchen. When the house was restored, it was abandoned and lived in by squatters. They left shortly after moving in under mysterious circumstances, including hearing strange noises from the attic.

Today the house is uninhabited, but a strange aura surrounds 193 Nieuwegracht.

Pictures have been taken then later figures are seen in the windows. Take your own and see for yourself!

# Walk from Haunted House to Kafe Belgie

**Transport Type:** Walk
**Time:** 05:30 pm ~ 05:40 pm

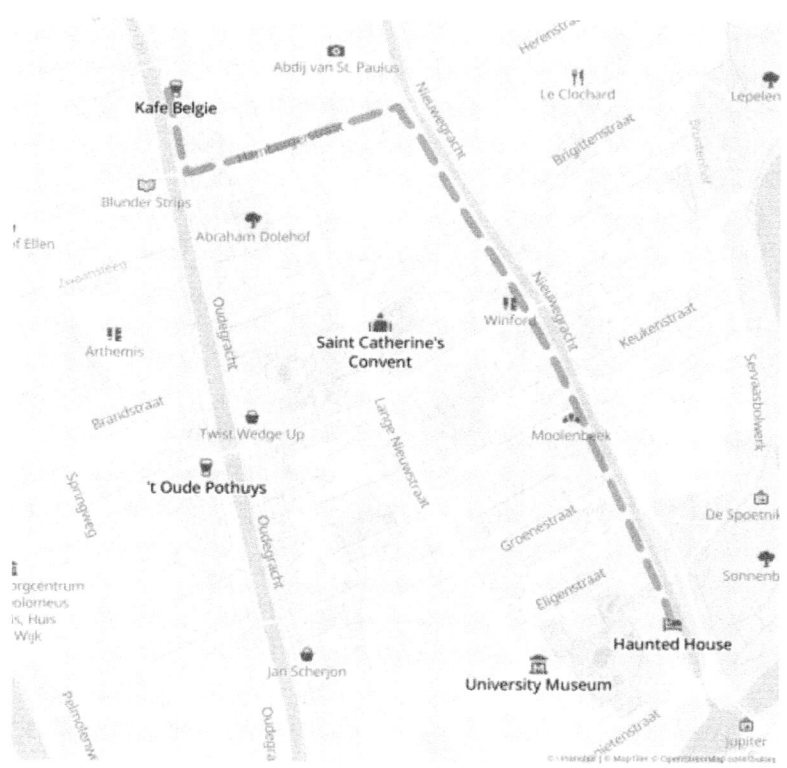

Continue along Nieuwegracht and left on Hamburgerstraat (hungry yet? ), turn right on the Oudegracht, it will look familiar from earlier on in the day. Kafe Belgie is on the right.

# Kafe Belgie

**Time:** 05:40 pm ~ 08:00 pm
**Type:** Restaurant / Cafe / Bar
**Cost:** €10.00
**Address:** Oudegracht 196

photo credit: Aly Coy

Try some of the Belgian beers on tap, my favourite is La Chouffe. With that one you will need some food in you, because it's pretty high percent in alcohol!

Kafe Belgie is a favourite for locals and for travellers. There is a complete mix of customers to match the range of beers sold! Try to get a spot outside in the sun. The menu consists of pub food, which is actually rare to find in Holland. Suggestions include garlic-butter toastie (like a grilled cheese), and Dutch fries with mayonnaise.

# Day 2

## Graffiti Wall by Central Station

**Time:** 09:30 am ~ 10:00 am
**Type:** Other
**Address:** Corner of Jaarbeursplein and Van Sijpesteijnkade

**How to get here:** It's a two minute walk from one of the exits of the central station called **Jaarbeursplein**. From Jaarbeursplein, from the perspective of coming down the escalator/stairs head right to get to the street. You will see NH hotel on the corner, and the graffiti tunnel is across from that.

The **graffiti tunnel** explains itself really, one thing to look out for is drawings of a lawn gnome. It's from a famous anonymous graffiti artist, who has drawn these gnomes scattered throughout the country! Great photo opportunities, just watch out for the bikers passing by.

## Walk from Graffiti Wall to Flea Market

**Transport Type:** Walk
**Time:** 10:00 am ~ 10:15 am

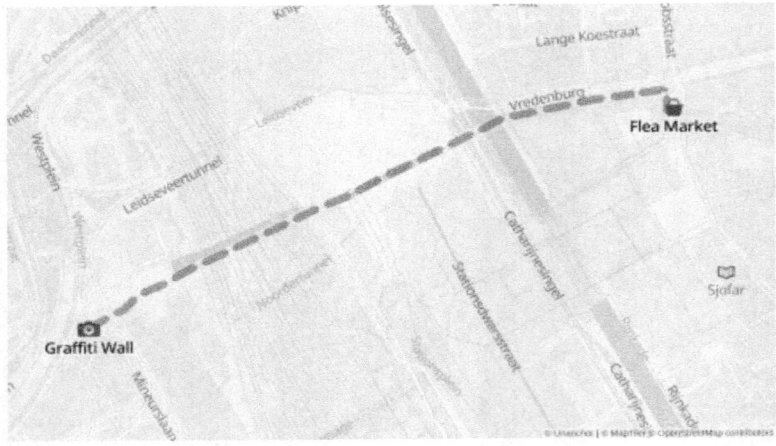

From heading through the graffiti tunnel and back to where you started, follow the road Van Sijpesteijnkade that heads through the tunnel. Out of the tunnel continue straight along Smakkelaarsveld until you see the market on your right hand side, you can't miss it.

# Flea Market

**Time:** 10:15 am ~ 11:15 am
**Type:** Market
**Address:** Fredenburg

photo credit: aly coy

This market is the largest in Utrecht and goes on every Wednesday, Friday and Saturday. There is just about everything sold, from freshly squeezed orange juice, home-made stroopwafels (a must eat), clothes, Dutch cheese, veggies, electrical equipment, to sewing supplies. On Fridays there is an organic market included amongst the stalls.

If you're travelling on a Monday, Tuesday, Thursday or Sunday, head to **Kanaalstraat**, where there are lots of Morroccon shops and cheap stores to buy fruit or veggies to keep you going along the tour. It's a very dynamic area where first only immigrants lived, then came the students, and now it's a very hip yet cheap place to live.

So instead of walking through the large tunnel to get to the city center, head back along Jaarbeursplein (but not into the bus area) and at first intersection take a right. You'll be on Damstraat, and first left is Kanaalstraat. Take a walk up and down that street and it will feel like you didn't miss the market at all!

# Flea market to Mariaplaats

**Transport Type:** Walk
**Time:** 11:15 am ~ 11:25 am

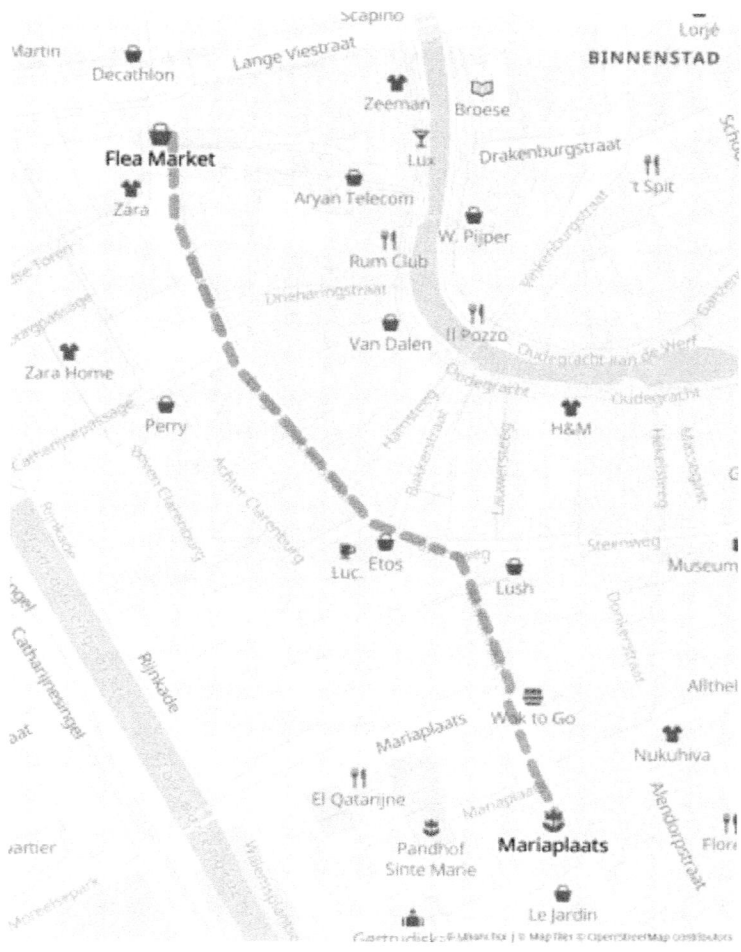

Walk along Lange Elisabethstraat which turns into Mariastraat. Mariaplaats is a little garden plaza on your left.

# Mariaplaats

**Time:** 11:25 am ~ 12:00 pm
**Type:** Park
**Address:** Mariaplaats

photo credit: aly coy

Mariaplaats is a nice quiet place to take a break and eat your stroopwaffel (the extra one you bought for your friend you're meeting later but will eat now without telling them). The herb garden in the middle has lavender, rosemary, sage and thyme amongst many other nice smelling herbs. There is a sign listing all that is there. Feel free to pick some to take with you, if no one is watching.

There used to be a homeless man who sat at Mariaplaats constantly, with his rickety table and chair, playing chess with whoever sat down.

The ladies running the garden decided to replace it with a stone picnic bench but alas, the man stopped coming and no one ever plays chess on it.

# Shopping Around Mariaplaats and Zadelstraat

**Transport Type:** Walk
**Time:** 12:00 pm ~ 12:30 pm

On Zadelstraat, there are a bunch of unique shops worth mentioning. Walking from Mariaplaats on your left there's an alternative book store called **Wijze Kater**. It has books on gardening, moon calenders, feng shui, herbal medicine etc. all the good ol' hippy stuff!

The next alleyway on the left has a small candle shop called **Happy Heart Candle**. It's run by a sweet man in a wheelchair who you might end up volunteering for, for the rest of your trip.

Getting back onto Zadelstraat, visit **Slamaat** pharmacy if you need any over the counter medicine. There they also have things from essential oil, to beer making kits, and herbal medicine.

The **De Groene Winkel** is an organic grocery store with very friendly staff. Buy some organic groceries if you want to have a picnic in Mariaplaats instead of having lunch at a cafe.

Once in a while there is a zelfgemaaktemarkt (**self made market**) on Zadelstraat close to Mariaplaats. Every stall has hand-crafted things, from clothes, jewellery, hats, and soap to coffee and cakes. To see when the next one is, go to this website: www.zelfgemaaktemarkt.nl (http://www.zelfgemaaktemarkt.nl)

After a bit of stocking up on supplies, head back to Mariaplaats and to the cafe for lunch.

# Mariaplaats to Lunch at Springhaver Cafe

**Transport Type:** Walk
**Time:** 12:30 pm ~ 12:40 pm

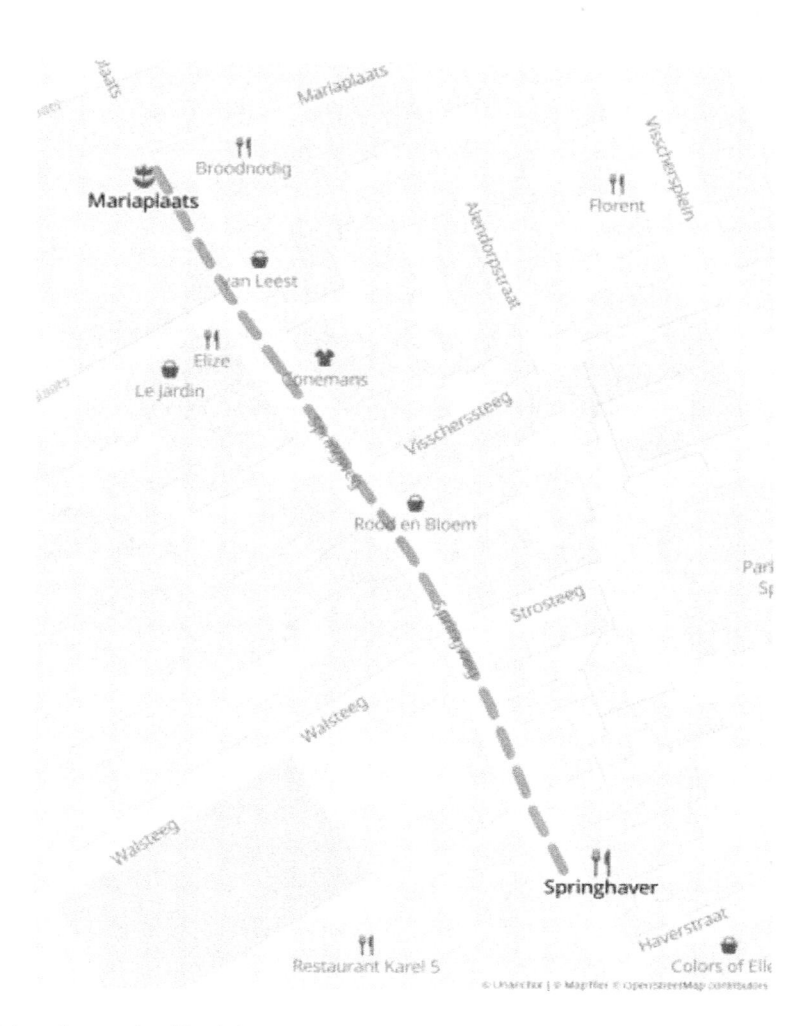

Walking from the Zadelstraat, when you hit Mariaplaats again turn left on Springweg, Springhaver is number 50.

# Lunch at Springhaver

**Time:** 12:40 pm ~ 02:00 pm
**Type:** Restaurant / Cafe / Bar
**Address:** Springweg 50

photo credit: aly coy

This cafe is also an independent movie theater (original language with Dutch subtitles) with the foyer since 1885.

For lunch, the cafe serves soups, sandwiches, omelettes and even things like a Mexican burrito. **Menu suggestion**: the chevre cheese with honey, thyme and walnuts on focaccia bread, and lemon and ginger tea.

**Price range:** €4-€7

# Springhaver to Centraal Museum

**Transport Type:** Walk
**Time:** 02:00 pm ~ 02:20 pm

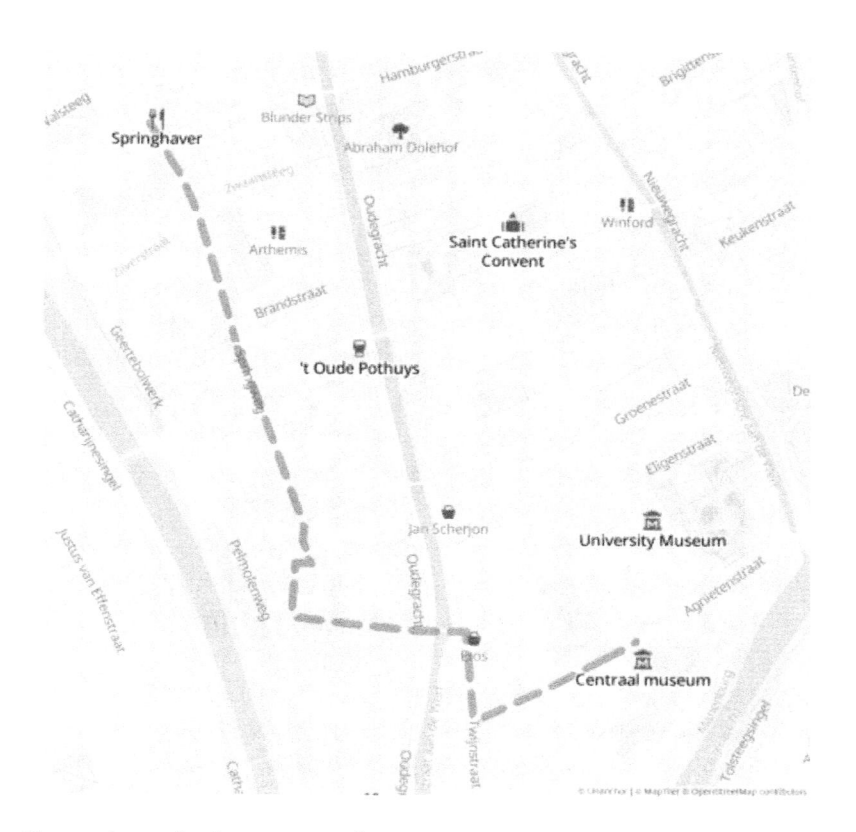

Continue along Springweg until you get to Lange Rozendaal. Take a left and head to the end of the street and cross over the bridge. Turn right on the first street over the bridge, Twijnstraat, then take the first left. Centraal Museum is on the right, and Dick Bruna Huis is on your left.

# Centraal Museum (incl. Dick Bruna Huis)

**Time:** 02:20 pm ~ 04:00 pm
**Type:** Museum
**Address:** Nicolaaskerkhof 10

The Centraal Museum has paintings, sculptures, architecture and ever-changing exhibits. It includes entrance into the dick bruna huis, the creator of 'Nijntje", or in English, Miffy. (See picture above). This exhibit has 7000 pieces including drawings, kids books, posters, and interactive games, perfect to bring kids, but also great for all ages.

Note that this museum is closed on Mondays.

# Centraal Museum to dinner at ACU

**Transport Type:** Walk
**Time:** 06:00 pm ~ 06:20 pm

## DAY 2

Take a slow stroll along the biggest canal in Utrecht, that surrounds the city center. It's away from tourists and very quiet. It's a good time to peak into the fancy houses that line the canal and take in the city.

Head right out of the museum to the large canal, just a two minute walk. Turn left and follow the canal all the way to Biltstraat and turn left, that street will turn into Voorstraat and the ACU is number 71.

If you want to take public transport, see directions below the maps.

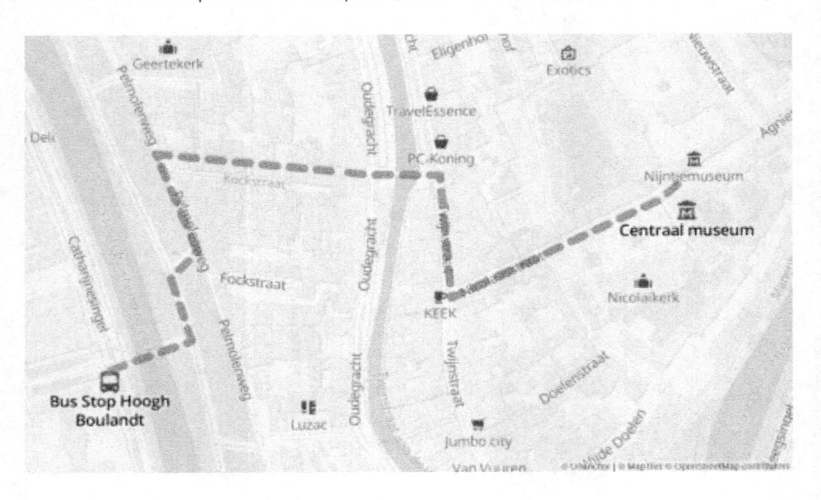

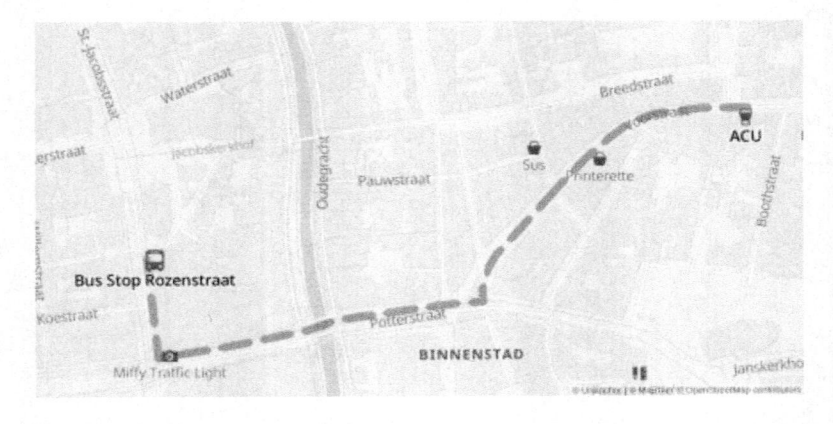

So, you're exhausted from walking around the museum. That's fine, you can take public transport to the next stop, dinner at the ACU.

Walk left out of the museum to Twijnstraat and turn right, take first bridge on left and head straight to the canal, turn left at the canal, cross over first bridge on right and you'll see the bus stop Hoogh Boulandt. Get off the bus at bus stop Rozenstraat. When you get off the bus walk towards the main street and turn left. You'll see a large square on your right called Neude. Voorstraat is on your left. Continue along the street until ACU at number 71.

For the bus schedule check out www.9292.nl (http://www.9292.nl) on your phone, cost of bus is €2.50

# Dinner at ACU

**Time:** 06:20 pm ~ 09:00 pm
**Type:** Restaurant / Cafe / Bar
**Address:** Voorstraat 71; 3512 AK Utrecht;

This squat turned restaurant/bar/club/political action meeting point, is vegetarian friendly and a great place to meet locals. They have activities almost every evening, whether it's a movie night, discussion on environmental issues, jam session or queer night, it's a cool place to see in Utrecht.

For the restaurant, every day there's a new vegetarian or vegan menu, costing €8.50. Nice food, nice people, cool vibe - good way to end your tour of Utrecht!

To make a reservation for dinner call 030-2314590, but it's not really necessary.

**Price range:** €8.50

# More Information

## Transportation, Money, and Useful Phrases

### Transportation tips

**Utrecht is a walkable city.** It's also nice by bike, but in the city center on a Saturday that gets a bit annoying and you end up walking your bike, running over people's feet etc etc. There are busses and trams that are easy to catch and very frequent, but to get to the heart of the city, is best done by foot.

*Local's Tip: Don't plan your tour day, or any tourist activity, on a Monday. Shops don't open until mid-day and museums aren't open at all.*

**If you are lost,** at every bus or tram stop there's a map of the city. And Dutch people are surprisingly good with directions, and English.

You can buy tram and bus tickets on the bus (they also will give change if you don't have exact) but for the train out of the city, you have to buy it before hand from a machine. At the desk, buying a ticket from a human costs 50 cents more.

On trains around the **country,** there's an option for a discount price of 40% but only if you have a Dutch discount card (student cards don't work). If you do find yourself with a discount ticket, ask the people sitting around you if they have a discount card, cardholders can take up to three people with them. (A good chance to meet the locals!)

## Some good websites to have on hand

**www.9292.nl (http://www.9292.nl)** From local busses, walking time to cross-country trips, this website will plan your route down to the minute. You can download the application to your phone. Available in English.

**www.ns.nl (http://www.ns.nl)** Just for train times and fares throughout the country. Also available in English.

**Note:** Taking a **Sprinter** train, doesn't mean what it implies. That is the **slow train**. **Inter-city** trains are the **fast** ones that don't stop at every tiny town along the way.

## Money – ATMs, credit cards & the currency

Your credit card must have a chip on it, and a password. If your card doesn't have this, go to your local bank to apply for one before you go abroad. Most places in Europe has this 'chip and pin' technology!

Currency is euros, nothing else will be accepted. Check http://www.xe.com/ (http://www.xe.com/) for the euro currency exchange. Personally, I find it better to just take money out from the ATMs instead of exchange at a currency exchange shop. They charge an extra processing fee and I always leave those places feeling ripped off. But, check with your bank if there are extra costs to take out cash.

## Getting into the City

From **Schipol airport to Utrecht Centraal,** the train goes every 15 minutes, and takes 30 mins to get there. (€7.90)

If you're flying with **RyanAir**, Eindhoven is closer to Utrecht than the other RyanAir airport Maastricht. Take the bus from the airport to

Eindhoven Centraal, then the train to Utrecht Centraal, taking about an hour in total. (€15)

From **Amsterdam Centraal**, it's about a 30 minute train and the trains go quite often. (€6.80)

## Useful Local Phrases

Everyone speaks English fluently but it's nice to know a couple words for common courtesy. Whatever you do- **don't speak German!**

Thank you very much: Dankuwel (Dunk-oo-vel)

Goodbye: Doei (doo-eyy) Almost sung in a high-pitched voice.

Delicious: Lekker (how it's written, and can be said for pretty much anything)

Have a nice meal: eet smakelijk (ate shmack-el-lick)

## National Holidays and Events

**Queen's Day is April 30th**, and is celebrating the Queen's birthday. Everyone wears orange and has the day off work, which means all day parties on boats, parks and outdoor stadiums. On this day anyone is allowed to sell things on the street, so it becomes a city-wide flea market!

**Note:** Book accommodation in advance, because the cities are packed. Also, don't plan to do the tour this day, everything's closed. If you shy away from crowds and public drunkenness, avoid this day like the plague!

# Restaurants, Hotels and Nightlife

## Restaurants

Eating etiquette isn't anything that outrageously different. The customer service isn't as good as in North America, but also tipping isn't as big. You can tip a small percentage (10 percent or less). It's not expected, but always appreciated.

A couple famous Dutch dishes are pancakes, split pea soup, **stroopwafels** (delicious thin waffles with caramel in the middle) and mashed potatoes, sausages and celery mixed together called **Stamppot**.

## Hotels

### Strowis

This backpacker's hostel is centrally located, includes a bar and helpful staff. There's a communal kitchen. Breakfast is not included. There are options to rent bikes from the place for €7 a day.

Boothstraat, corner of Neude Janskerkhof en Domplein, www.strowis.nl (http://www.strowis.nl)

### Fort aan de Klop

This old fort is a place just outside the city center for camping, or staying at the Inn. There is also a bar and all facilities. Suitable for large groups. Camping is only from April to September.

First Polderweg 4, www.fortaandeklop.com (http://www.fortaandeklop.com)

### B&B Hotel

This hotel is very relaxed and chaotic at the same time. The cost includes **free breakfast, lunch and dinner!** There are musical instruments to use, a big TV with movie selection, free wifi, nice staff and clients. It's in the city center and has no curfew.

Lucasbolwerk 4, www.hostelutrecht.nl (http://www.hostelutrecht.nl)

## Nightlife

**Tivoli** is a great music venue with different acts almost every night of the week. Check the website, or the big poster hanging out front to see who's playing. Tivoli is the place in Utrecht for well known acts and indie stuff. Also look for the international student nights!

www.tivoli.nl (http://www.tivoli.nl)

Oudegracht 245

**Vechtclub** is definitely a place to meet locals, it's out of the city center in a warehouse type venue that doubles as a theatre. Parties are thrown a couple times a month, but if you get a chance to go, it will take you far from tourist land!

www.vechtclub.nl (http://www.vechtclub.nl)

Brailledreef 9

# Other places to see

### Sterrenborgh

The Star Museum's observatory every Friday and Saturday from 7:30-9, September through to mid-April. If you like star gazing, this is the place for you! **www.sonnenborgh.nl (http://www.sonnenborgh.nl)**

## Lombok

The area of **Lombok**, is located on **Kanaalstraat**, on the other side of the central station coming from the city center. This area is very multicultural and is where the first immigrants lived in Utrecht. Now it's filled with a mix of students and is rich in culture. Here is where the cheapest vegetable shops are and where you can eat Mexican, Indonesian, Thai, Moroccan and the like.

OTHER PLACES TO SEE

# Our Story

Travellers can always recognize one another, and so it was us. We started travelling before we were married and simply never stopped.

Unanchor is our way to helping other experience the world in the same way that brought us so much joy.

# Keep in Touch

## Help us keep this guide up to date

We make every effort to make sure the facts and information in this itinerary are accurate and up to date. However, changes can and will occur. (This is part of what makes travel so interesting, of course.) This can be something as small as a phone number or hours of operations changing, or as significant as a new attraction opening.

We would love to hear from you if you notice any discrepancies in the itinerary, or if you have any suggestions on how to improve. All comments and suggestions will be communicated to the author and included in our regular updating process.

**Please send any and all feedback to hello@unanchor.com.**

Thank you and happy travelling!

Cheers,
Erin and Todd

# Other Unanchor Itineraries

## Africa

Cape Town - What Not to Miss on a 4 Day First-Timers' Itinerary
Johannesburg/Pretoria - Johannesburg/Pretoria: A 4-Day South Africa Tour Itinerary
Tangier - One Day in Africa - A Guide to Tangier

## Asia

Beijing - Beijing Must Sees, Must Dos, Must Eats - 3-Day Tour Itinerary
Bishkek - 4 Days in Bishkek on a Budget
Delhi - 3-Day Budget Delhi Itinerary
Delhi - Delhi in 3 Days - A Journey Through Time
Gapyeong - 3 Days in the Vibrant City of Seoul and the Serene Countryside of Gapyeong
Kolkata - Day Tryst with 300 Year-Old Kolkata
Kolkata - Kolkata (Calcutta): 2 Days of Highlights
Moscow - The Very Best of Moscow in 3 Days
Mumbai - 3 Days Highlights of Mumbai
Narita - Tour Narita During an Airport Layover
Nozawa - Nozawa Onsen's Winter Secrets - A 3-Day Tour
Saint Petersburg  - Saint Petersburg in Three Days
Shanghai - 2 Days in Shanghai: A Budget-Conscious Peek at Modern China
Tokyo - 3-Day Highlights of Tokyo
Ulaanbaatar - A First Timer's Weekend Guide to Ulaanbaatar

## Central America and the Caribbean

Dutch Sint Maarten - Two Exciting Days in Dutch Sint Maarten - Hello Cruisers!
San Juan - Old San Juan, Puerto Rico 2-Day Walking Itinerary
St. Croix - Two Amazing Days in St. Croix, USVI - Hello Cruisers!

## Europe

Amsterdam - Amsterdam 3-Day Alternative Tour: Not just the Red Light District
Amsterdam - Amsterdam Made Easy: A 3-Day Guide
Belgrade - Belgrade: 7 Days of History on Foot
Berlin - 2 Days In Berlin On A Budget
Berlin - A 3-Day Guide to Berlin, Germany
Braşov - Braşov: Feel the Pulse of Transylvania in 3 Days
Brussels - 3 Days in Brussels - The Grand Sites Via the Path Less Trodden
Budapest - Highlights of Budapest in 3 Days
Copenhagen - 3 Days in Copenhagen - Explore Like a Local
Copenhagen - Best of Copenhagen 2-Day Walking Itinerary
Copenhagen - Christmas in Copenhagen - A 2-Day Guide
Dublin - 3 Days in Dublin City - City Highlights, While Eating & Drinking Like a Local
Helsinki - 3 Days in Helsinki
Iceland - Beginner's Iceland - A 4-Day Self-Drive Itinerary
Krakow - Krakow: 3-Day Tour of Poland's Cultural Capital
Lausanne - Lausanne 1-Day Tour Itinerary
Lisbon - Lisbon in 3 Days: Budget Itinerary
Moldova - 3 Days of Fresh Air in Moldova's Countryside
Mostar - A City with Soul in 1 Day
Prague - 3-Day Prague Beer Pilgrimage

Prague - Best of Prague - 3-Day Itinerary
Tbilisi - Weekend Break: Tbilisi - Crown Jewel of the Caucasus
Utrecht - 2-Day Tour of Utrecht: The Smaller, Less Touristy Amsterdam!
Warsaw - Best of Warsaw 2-Day Itinerary
Zagreb - Zagreb For Art Lovers: A Three-Day Itinerary

# France

Chartres - Paris to Chartres Cathedral: 1-Day Tour Itinerary
Mont St Michel - A 3-Day Tour of Mont St Michel, Normandy and Brittany
Paris - Art Lovers' Paris: A 2-Day Artistic Tour of the City of Lights
Paris - Paris 1-Day Itinerary - Streets of Montmartre
Paris - Paris 3-Day Walking Tour: See Paris Like a Local
Paris - Paris 4-Day Winter Wonderland
Paris - Paris for Free: 3 Days
Paris - The Best of Paris in One Day
Paris - Paris Foodie Classics: 1 Day of French Food

# Greece

Athens - Athens 3-Day Highlights Tour Itinerary
Chania & Sfakia - Chania & Sfakia, Greece & Great Day Trips Nearby (5-Day Itinerary)
Halkidiki - 2-Day Beach Tour: Travel like a Local in Sithonia Peninsula, Halkidiki, Greece
Halkidiki - Day Trip From Thessaloniki to Kassandra Peninsula, Halkidiki, Greece
Santornini - Santorini, Greece in 3 Days: Living like a Local
Thessaloniki - Thessaloniki, Greece - 3-Day Highlights Itinerary

## Italy

Florence - 3-Day Florence Walking Tours
Florence - Florence, Italy 3-Day Art & Culture Itinerary
Lake Como - A Day on Lake Como, Italy
Milan - Milan Unknown - A 3-day tour itinerary
Puglia - Landscape, Food, & Trulli: 1 Week in Puglia, the Valle d'Itria, and Matera
Rome - 3 Days of Roman Adventure: Spending Time and Money Efficiently in Rome
Rome - A 3-Day Tour Around Ancient Rome
Rome - Discover Rome's Layers: A 3-Day Walking Tour
Siena - See Siena in a Day
Venice - Three Romantic Walks in Venice

## Spain

Barcelona - 3-Day Highlights of Barcelona Itinerary
Barcelona - FC Barcelona: More than a Club (A 1-Day Experience)
Ibiza - Ibiza on a Budget - 3 -Day Itinerary
Logroño -  Three days exploring Logroño and La Rioja by Public Transport
Málaga -  Málaga, Spain – 2-Day Tour from the Moors to Picasso
Mijas - Mijas - One Day Tour of an Andalucían White Village
Seville - Two-Day Tour in Sunny Seville, Spain
Valencia - Best of Valencia 2-Day Guide

## United Kingdom

Bath - Bath: An Exploring Guide - 2-Day Itinerary
Belfast - History, Culture, and Craic: 3 Days in Belfast, Ireland
Brighton - 2-Day Brighton Best-of Walks & Activities
Bristol - Bristol in 2 Days: A Local's Guide

Cardiff - Two-Day Self-Guided Walks - Cardiff
Edinburgh - The Best of Edinburgh: A 3-Day Journey from Tourist to Local
London - 3-Day London Tour for Olympic Visitors
London - An Insider's Guide to the Best of London in 3 Days
London - Done London? A 3-day itinerary for off the beaten track North Norfolk
London - London 1-Day Literary Highlights
London - London for Free :: Three-Day Tour
London - London's Historic City Wall Walk (1-2 days)
London - London's South Bank - Off the Beaten Track 1-Day Tour
London - London's Villages - A 3-day itinerary exploring Hampstead, Marylebone and
London - Notting Hill, Low-Cost, Luxury London - 3-Day Itinerary
London - The 007 James Bond Day Tour of London
Manchester - MADchester - A Local's 3-Day Guide To Manchester
Margate - One Day in Margate, UK on a Budget

# Middle East

Amman - Adventure Around Amman: A 2-Day Itinerary
Amman - Amman 2-Day Cultural Tour
Doha - Doha 2-Day Stopover Cultural Tour
Doha - Doha Surf and Turf: A two-day itinerary
Istanbul - 3 Days as an Istanbulite: An Istanbul Itinerary
Istanbul - Between the East and the West, a 3-Day Istanbul Itinerary
Paphos - Paphos 3-Day Itinerary: Live like a local!

# North America

## Canada

Halifax - Relax in Halifax for Two Days Like a Local
Toronto - An Insider's Guide to Toronto: Explore the City Less Traveled in Three Days
Toronto - The Best of Toronto - 2-Day Itinerary
Toronto - Toronto: A Multicultural Retreat (3-day itinerary)

## Mexico

Cancun - Cancun and Mayan Riviera 5-Day Itinerary (3rd Edition)
Mexico City - Everything to see or do in Mexico City - 7-Day Itinerary
Mexico City - Mexico City 3-Day Highlights Itinerary
Mexico City - Todo Lo Que Hay Que Ver o Hacer en la Ciudad de México - Itinerario de 7 Días
Chiapas - Your Chiapas Adventure: San Cristobal de las Casas and Palenque, Mexico 5-Day Itinerary

## United States

### East Coast

Asheville - Girls' 3-Day Weekend Summer Getaway in Asheville, NC
Atlanta - Atlanta 3-Day Highlights
Baltimore - Baltimore: A Harbor, Parks, History, Seafood & Art - 3-Day Itinerary
Boston - Boston 2-Day Historic Highlights Itinerary
Boston - Navigating Centuries of Boston's Nautical History in One Day
Boston - Rainy Day Boston One-Day Itinerary

# NORTH AMERICA

Brooklyn - Brooklyn, NY 2-Day Foodie Tour
Burlington - The Weekenders Guide To Burlington, Vermont
Hamptons - A Local's Guide to the Hamptons 3-Day Itinerary
Hudson River - Day Trek Along the Hudson River
Hudson Valley - Day Trip from New York City: Heights of the Hudson Valley (Bridges and
Ridges)
Key West - 2 Days Exploring Haunted Key West
Lancaster County - 3 Day PA Dutch Country Highlights (Lancaster County, PA)ta
Montauk - A Local's Guide to Montauk, New York in 2 Days - From the Ocean to the Hills
New Haven - New Haven Highlights: Art, Culture & History 3-Day Itinerary
New York City - Day Trip from New York City: Mountains, Falls, & a Funky Town
New York City - 3-Day Amazing Asian Food Tour of New York City!
New York City - Weekend Day Trip from New York City: The Wine & Whiskey Trail
New York City - Hidden Bars of New York City's East Village & Lower East Side: A 2-Evening
Itinerary
New York City - Jewish New York in Two Days
New York City - Lower Key, Lower Cost: Lower Manhattan - 1-Day Itinerary
New York City - New York City - First Timer's 2-Day Walking Tour
New York City - New York City's Lower East Side, 1-Day Tour Itinerary
New York City - New York Like A Native: Five Boroughs in Six Days
Orlando - 3-Day Discover Orlando Itinerary
Outer Banks - Five Days in the Wild Outer Banks of North Carolina
Philadelphia - Two Days in Philadelphia
Pittsburgh - Pittsburgh: Three Days Off the Beaten Path
Richmond - RVA Haunts, History, and Hospitality: Three Days in

Richmond, Virginia
Savannah - Savannah 3-Day Highlights Itinerary
St. Petersburg - Three Days in the Sunshine City of St. Petersburg, Florida
Washington, DC - Washington, DC in 4 Days
Washington, DC - Washington, DC: 3 Days Like a Local

## Central US

Austin - A Laid-Back Long Weekend in Austin, TX
Chicago - 3-Day Chicago Highlights Itinerary
Chicago - 6-Hour "Layover" Chicago
Chicago - Chicago Food, Art and Funky Neighborhoods in 3 Days
Chicago - Famous Art & Outstanding Restaurants in Chicago 1-Day Itinerary
Columbus - Family Weekend in Columbus, OH
Columbus - Ohio State Game Day Weekend
Corpus Christi - Corpus Christi: The Insider Guide for a 4-Day Tour
Kansas City - The Best of Kansas City: 3-Day Itinerary
La Grange - La Grange, Kentucky: A 3-Day Tour Itinerary
Louisville - Louisville: Three Days in Derby City
New Orleans - New Orleans 3-Day Itinerary
Wichita - Wichita From Cowtown to Air Capital in 2 Days

## West Coast

Alaska - Alaska Starts Here - 3 Days in Seward
Asbury - Cruisin' Asbury like a Local in 1 Day
Bainbridge Island - A Day on Bainbridge Island
Beverly Hills - Beverly Hills, Los Angeles - 1-Day Tour
Big Island - Tackling 10 Must-Dos on the Big Island in 3 Days
Boulder - The Best of Boulder, CO: A Three-Day Guide
Central Coast - Three Days in Central California's Wine Country

# NORTH AMERICA

Jackson Hole - Summer in Jackson Hole: Local Tips for the Perfect Three to Five Day Adventure

Las Vegas - Las Vegas - Gaming Destination Diversions - Ultimate 3-Day Itinerary

Las Vegas - Las Vegas on a Budget - 3-Day Itinerary

Los Angeles - 2-Day Los Angeles Vegan and Vegetarian Foodie Itinerary

Los Angeles - Downtown Los Angeles 1-Day Walking Tour

Los Angeles - Hollywood, Los Angeles - 1-Day Walking Tour

Los Angeles - Sunset Strip, Los Angeles - 1-Day Walking Tour

Los Angeles - Los Angeles 4-Day Itinerary (partly using Red Tour Bus)

Los Angeles - Los Angeles Highlights 3-Day Itinerary

Los Angeles - Los Angeles On A Budget - 4-Day Tour Itinerary

Moab - An Active 2-3 Days In Moab, Utah

Napa Valley - Beyond the Vine: 2-Day Napa Tour

Napa Valley - Wine, Food, and Fun: 3 Days in Napa Valley

Northern California - Beer Lovers 3-Day Guide To Northern California

Oahu - Lesser-known Oahu in 4 Days on a Budget

Oahu - Local's Guide to Oahu - 3-Day Tour Itinerary

Orange County - Orange County 3-Day Budget Itinerary

Palm Springs - Palm Springs, Joshua Tree & Salton Sea: A 3-Day Itinerary

Portland - Portland Bike and Bite: A 2-Day Itinerary

Portland - Three Days Livin' as a True and Local Portlander

Portland - Weekend Tour of Portland's Craft Breweries, Wineries, & Distilleries

San Diego - Best of the Best: Three-Day San Diego Itinerary

San Francisco 2-Day Highlights Itinerary

San Francisco Foodie Weekend Itinerary

Silicon Valley - The Tech Lover's 48-Hour Travel Guide to Silicon Valley & San Francisco

Tucson - Tucson: 3 Days at the Intersection of Mexico, Native America & the Old West

## Oceania

Blue Mountains (Sydney) - The Blue Mountains: A weekend of nature, culture and history.
Christchurch - Enjoy the Rebuild - Christchurch 2-Day Tour
Melbourne - A Weekend Snapshot of Melbourne
Melbourne - An Afternoon & Evening in Melbourne's Best Hidden Bars
Melbourne - Laneway Melbourne: A One-Day Walking Tour
Melbourne - Magic of Melbourne 3-Day Tour
Newcastle - Two Wheels and Pair of Cozzies: the Best of Newcastle in 3 Days
Perth - Best of Perth's Most Beautiful Sights in 3 Days
Sydney - A Weekend Snapshot of Sydney
Sydney - Sydney, Australia - 3-Day **Best Of** Itinerary
Wellington - The Best of Wellington: 3-Day Itinerary

## South America

Arequipa - A 1-Day Foodie's Dream Tour of Arequipa
Arequipa - Arequipa - A 2-Day Itinerary for First-Time Visitors
Buenos Aires - An Insider's Guide to the Best of Buenos Aires in 3 Days
Buenos Aires - Buenos Aires Best Kept Secrets: 2-Day Itinerary
Cuenca - Cuenca, Ecuador - A 3-Day Discovery Tour
Cusco - Cusco and the Sacred Valley - a five-day itinerary for a first-time visitor
Lima - Little Known Lima 3-Day Tour
São Paulo - Sights & Sounds of São Paulo - 3-Day Itinerary

# Southeast Asia

Bangkok - Girls' Weekend in Bangkok: Shop, Spa, Savour, Swoon
Bangkok - The Ins and Outs of Bangkok: A 3-Day Guide
Borobudur - Go with the Sun to Borobudur & Prambanan in 1 Day
Hong Kong - Between the Skyscrapers - Hong Kong 3-Day Discovery Tour
Kaohsiung- The Two Worlds of Kaohsiung in 5 Days
Manila - A 3-Day Thrilla in Manila then Flee to the Sea
Manila - Manila on a Budget: 2-Day Itinerary
Saigon - Saigon 3-Day Beyond the Guidebook Itinerary
Singapore- A First Timer's Guide to 3 Days in the City that Barely Sleeps - Singapore
Singapore - Family Friendly Singapore - 3 Days in the Lion City
Singapore - Singapore: 3 Fun-Filled Days on this Tiny Island
Singapore - The Affordable Side of Singapore: A 4-Day Itinerary
Taipei - 72 Hours in Taipei: The All-rounder
Ubud, Bali - Art and Culture in Ubud, Bali – 1-Day Highlights

# UNANCHOR

*Unanchor is a global family for travellers to experience the world with the heart of a local.*

Printed in Great Britain
by Amazon